Millie Ola Children's Book Series

Says OlaRose

1 1 1 2 3 3

By Olachi Mezu-Ndubuisi

BLACK ACADEMY PRESS, INC.

_____

_____

_____

_____

_____

_____

_____

_____

_____

_____

_____

OLACHI MEZU NDUBUISI   1, 2, 3 SAYS OLAROSE

Millie Ola Children's Book Series

Says OlaRose
By Olachi Mezu-Ndubuisi
BLACK ACADEMY PRESS, INC.
4015 Old Court Road, Pikesville, Maryland 21208

Copyright ©2016 Black Academy Press Inc.
Written and created by Olachi Mezu Ndubuisi
Illustrated by Cam

First Published in USA in 2009
By Black Academy Press, Inc.
www.blackacademypress.com
2nd edition printed in 2016
1,2,3 Says OlaRose and The Millie Ola Children's Book Collection are trademarks of
Black Academy Press, Inc. All rights reserved.

Printed in the U.S.A
ISBN: 0-87831-141-6 978-0-87831-141-5

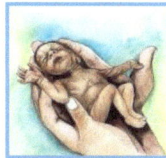

Book sales will go to the ObiOlaRose Twin Angels Foundation to help
support parents of premature and sick infants and neonatal services in
underserved areas.
www.obiolarosefoundation.org

Dedication

To my miracle baby, OlaRose, who was born early. You are my inspiration, source of strength, and God's most precious gift to me.

This book belongs to

_____

Please read it to me.

1 bird flying.
Along comes 1,
and there are 2 birds
flying high up in the sky.

2 babies playing.
Along comes 1,
and there are 3 babies
playing on the floor

3 boats sailing.

Along comes 1,

and there are 4 boats

sailing in the water.

4 horses racing.

Along comes 1,

and there are 5 horses racing

through the woods

5 sheep grazing.

Along comes 1,

and   there   are   6   sheep

grazing in the grass.

6 Mommies drinking.

Along comes 1,

and there are 7 mommies

drinking some tea.

7 Daddies playing.

Along comes 1,

and there are 8

daddies

playing with the ball

8 peas laying

along comes 1,

and there are 9

peas laying

ready to eat

9 fingers resting

along comes 1,

and there are 10 fingers

resting on my hands.

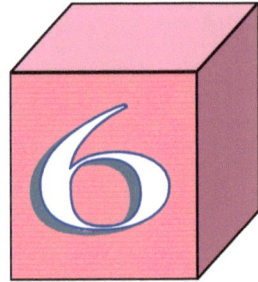

Millie Ola Children's Book Series

I know my 1, 2, 3
I know my numbers
I know my 1, 2, 3 to 10
Do you know your 1, 2, 3
Says OlaRose

Millie Ola Children's Book Series

About the Book

1,2,3 Says OlaRose is one of the books in the Says OlaRose Collection of the Millie Ola Children's Book Series.

About The Author

Olachi Mezu-Ndubuisi *aka* Millie Ola is an optometrist, neonatologist, research scientist and mother of premature one pound daughter, OlaRose, who uses her love for writing to follow, nurture and cherish her daughter's development.

Book sales will go to the ObiOlaRose Twin Angels Foundation to help support parents of premature and sick infants and neonatal services in underserved areas.

www.obiolarosefoundation.org

9 780878 311415